froglets

Learners

Bears

by Annabelle Lynch

First published in 2014 by
Franklin Watts
338 Euston Road
London NW1 3BH

Franklin Watts Australia
Level 17/207 Kent Street
Sydney NSW 2000

Picture credits: Antoine Beyeler/Dreamstime: 6. Steve
Bower/Shutterstock: 11. Hung Chung Chih/
Shutterstock: front cover, 19. Erik Mandre/
Shutterstock: 8, 12, 20-21. Gerard Marella/
Shutterstock: 4. Jez Perklauzen/istockphoto: 5.
Photobulb/Dreamstime: 15. Yvonne Pijnenburg-
Schonewille/Shutterstock: 17. Martin Shields/Alamy:
14. Sergey Uryadnikov/Shutterstock: 1, 16.

Every attempt has been made to clear copyright.
Should there be any inadvertent omission please
apply to the publisher for rectification.

A CIP catalogue record for this book is
available from the British Library.

Dewey number: 428.6

ISBN 978 1 4451 2911 2 (hbk)
ISBN 978 1 4451 3044 6 (pbk)
Library eBook ISBN 978 1 4451 2917 4

Series Editor: Julia Bird
Series Advisor: Catherine Glavina
Series Designer: Peter Scoulding

Printed in China

Franklin Watts is a division of Hachette Children's Books,
an Hachette UK company. www.hachette.co.uk

Contents

The words in **bold** can be found in the glossary.

What are bears?

Bears are big, furry animals. They are found all over the world. They live in hot **rainforests**, cool mountains and icy shores.

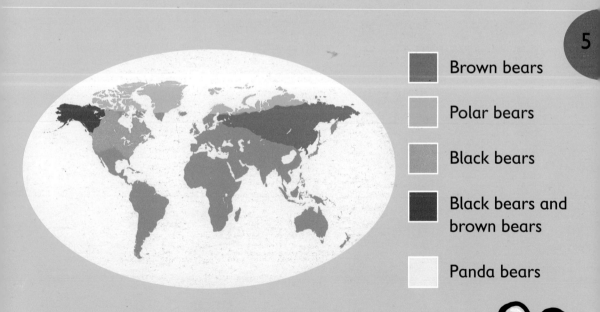

Brown bears

Polar bears

Black bears

Black bears and brown bears

Panda bears

What do bears look like?

Bears all have thick fur, strong legs with big paws, a long **snout** and a short tail. Bears also have sharp teeth and claws.

A polar bear's thick fur helps to protect it from the cold.

Brown bears

Brown bears are found in deep forests and high **mountains**.

They are big and heavy, but they can move quickly to catch their **prey**.

Brown bears eat all sorts of food, from nuts and berries to fish and insects.

Sleepy bears

Every winter, brown bears find a dark cave or dig a hole under a tree. They rest there for a long time. This is called hibernating.

Bear babies

Bear babies are called cubs. Brown bear cubs are born in winter. The mother bear finds a safe, warm place called a den to give birth.

Bear cubs stay close to their mother for two years or more.

Black bears

Black bears are found deep in the forests of North America. They are good at climbing and love hiding up in trees.

Black bears are often found eating out of rubbish bins!

Polar bears

Polar bears live on the icy
shores of the Arctic
Ocean. They are great
swimmers and spend
most of their life at sea,
looking for seals to eat.

A polar bear can smell
a seal from nearly one
kilometre away.

Pandas

Giant pandas love to eat a plant called bamboo. They live in the cool mountain forests in China where bamboo grows.

Giant pandas are some of the **rarest** animals in the world.

Bears at risk

We must **protect** bears. People **hunt** them for their fur. The forests where they live are also being cut down.

Bears in the wild:
Black bears: 1 million
Brown bears: over 200,000
Polar bears: 20–25,000
Giant pandas: 1,000

Glossary

hunt – to track down and kill an animal

mountain – a high area of land with steep sides

prey – an animal eaten by another animal

protect – to look after

rainforest – thick forest with tall trees

rare – something that is not often seen

snout – a bear's nose and mouth

Websites:

http://kids.nationalgeographic.com/kids/animals/creaturefeature/brown-bear/

http://kids.sandiegozoo.org/animals/mammals/polar-bear

Every effort has been made by the Publishers to ensure that the websites are suitable for children, and that they contain no inappropriate or offensive material. However, because of the nature of the Internet, it is impossible to guarantee that the contents of these sites will not be altered. We strongly advise that Internet access is supervised by a responsible adult.

Quiz

1. Where are brown bears found?

2. When do brown bears hibernate?

3. What are bear babies called?

4. Where do polar bears live?

5. What do giant pandas eat?

6. What do people hunt bears for?

The answers are on page 24

Answers

1. Deep forests and high mountains
2. Winter
3. Cubs
4. On the shores of the Arctic Ocean
5. Bamboo
6. Fur

Index